Norris

by Iain Gray

PUBLISHING

WRITING *to* REMEMBER

79 Main Street, Newtongrange,
Midlothian EH22 4NA
Tel: 0131 344 0414   Fax: 0845 075 6085
E-mail: info@lang-syne.co.uk
www.langsyneshop.co.uk

Design by Dorothy Meikle
Printed by Blissetts
© Lang Syne Publishers Ltd 2021

All rights reserved. No part of this publication may be reproduced, stored or introduced into a retrieval system, or transmitted in any form or by any means (electronic, mechanical, photocopying, recording or otherwise) without the prior written permission of Lang Syne Publishers Ltd.

ISBN 978-1-85217-792-8

Norris

MOTTO:
Faithfully serve

CREST:
A raven

TERRITORY:
Berkshire and Lancashire

NAME variations include:
- Norres
- Norrie
- Norreys
- Norrice
- Norrish

Chapter one:

The origins of popular surnames

by George Forbes and Iain Gray

***If you don't know where you came from, you won't know where you're going** is a frequently quoted observation and one that has a particular resonance today when there has been a marked upsurge in interest in genealogy, with increasing numbers of people curious to trace their family roots.*

Main sources for genealogical research include census returns and official records of births, marriages and deaths – and the key to unlocking the detail they contain is obviously a family surname, one that has been 'inherited' and passed from generation to generation.

No matter our station in life, we all have a surname – but it was not until about the middle of the fourteenth century that the practice of being identified by a particular surname became commonly established throughout the British Isles.

Previous to this, it was normal for a person to be identified through the use of only a forename.

But as population gradually increased and there were many more people with the same forename, surnames were adopted to distinguish one person, or community, from another.

Many common English surnames are patronymic in origin, meaning they stem from the forename of one's father – with 'Johnson,' for example, indicating 'son of John.'

It was the Normans, in the wake of their eleventh century conquest of Anglo-Saxon England, a pivotal moment in the nation's history, who first brought surnames into usage – although it was a gradual process.

For the Normans, these were names initially based on the title of their estates, local villages and chateaux in France to distinguish and identify these landholdings.

Such grand descriptions also helped enhance the prestige of these warlords and generally glorify their lofty positions high above the humble serfs slaving away below in the pecking order who had only single names, often with Biblical connotations as in Pierre and Jacques.

The only descriptive distinctions among the peasantry concerned their occupations, like 'Pierre the swineherd' or 'Jacques the ferryman.'

Roots of surnames that came into usage in England not only included Norman-French, but also Old French, Old Norse, Old English, Middle English, German, Latin, Greek, Hebrew and the Gaelic languages of the Celts.

The Normans themselves were originally Vikings, or 'Northmen', who raided, colonised and eventually settled down around the French coastline.

They had sailed up the Seine in their longboats in 900AD under their ferocious leader Rollo and ruled the roost in north eastern France before sailing over to conquer England in 1066 under Duke William of Normandy – better known to posterity as William the Conqueror, or King William I of England.

Granted lands in the newly-conquered England, some of their descendants later acquired territories in Wales, Scotland and Ireland – taking not only their own surnames, but also the practice of adopting a surname, with them.

But it was in England where Norman rule and custom first impacted, particularly in relation to the adoption of surnames.

This is reflected in the famous *Domesday Book*, a massive survey of much of England and Wales, ordered by William I, to determine who owned what, what it was worth and therefore how much they were liable to pay in taxes to the voracious Royal Exchequer.

Completed in 1086 and now held in the National Archives in Kew, London, 'Domesday' was an Old English word meaning 'Day of Judgement.'

This was because, in the words of one contemporary chronicler, "its decisions, like those of the Last Judgement, are unalterable."

It had been a requirement of all those English landholders – from the richest to the poorest – that they identify themselves for the purposes of the survey and for future reference by means of a surname.

This is why the *Domesday Book*, although written in Latin as was the practice for several centuries with both civic and ecclesiastical records, is an invaluable source for the early appearance of a wide range of English surnames.

Several of these names were coined in connection with occupations.

These include Baker and Smith, while Cooks, Chamberlains, Constables and Porters were to be found carrying out duties in large medieval households.

The church's influence can be found in names such as Bishop, Friar and Monk while the popular name of Bennett derives from the late fifth to mid-sixth century Saint Benedict, founder of the Benedictine order of monks.

The early medical profession is represented by Barber, while businessmen produced names that include Merchant and Sellers.

Down at the village watermill, the names that cropped up included Millar/Miller, Walker and Fuller, while other self-explanatory trades included Cooper, Tailor, Mason and Wright.

Even the scenery was utilised as in Moor, Hill, Wood and Forrest – while the hunt and the chase supplied names that include Hunter, Falconer, Fowler and Fox.

Colours are also a source of popular surnames, as in Black, Brown, Gray/Grey, Green and White, and would have denoted the colour of the clothing the person habitually wore or, apart from the obvious exception of 'Green', one's hair colouring or even complexion.

The surname Red developed into Reid, while

Blue was rare and no-one wanted to be associated with yellow.

Rather self-important individuals took surnames that include Goodman and Wiseman, while physical attributes crept into surnames such as Small and Little.

Many families proudly boast the heraldic device known as a Coat of Arms, as featured on our front cover.

The central motif of the Coat of Arms would originally have been what was borne on the shield of a warrior to distinguish himself from others on the battlefield.

Not featured on the Coat of Arms, but highlighted on page three, is the family motto and related crest – with the latter frequently different from the central motif.

Adding further variety to the rich cultural heritage that is represented by surnames is the appearance in recent times in lists of the 100 most common names found in England of ones that include Khan, Patel and Singh – names that have proud roots in the vast sub-continent of India.

Echoes of a far distant past can still be found in our surnames and they can be borne with pride in commemoration of our forebears.

Chapter two:

Royal favour

A name with a number of points of origin, 'Norris' and its popular spelling variant 'Norreys' features prominently in the historical record.

One source is the Middle English *norais*, *noreis* or *norries*, indicating 'northerner' and thought to have denoted a person who hailed from the north of England or, even further afield, Scandinavia.

As a topographical name it denoted someone who lived on the north side of an estate while, in an occupational sense and derived from the Middle English *norice* or Old French *norrice*, it meant 'nurse' or 'foster parent'.

It was in the wake of the Norman Conquest of 1066, a pivotal event in British history, when one prominent family of the name became established in the English country of Berkshire and also later in Lancashire, that they first appear on official records – and the fact that they do so indicates they were worthy of note.

The *Domesday Book*, referred to in the previous chapter, names the Berkshire parish and village of 'Hanstede' which, in 1448, changed its name to Hampstede Norreys when a Norreys family bought the manor.

Now known as Hampstead Norreys and centred on a small tributary of the River Penn, north of Newbury, it is noted today for the ruins of a Norman castle and parish church from the same era.

A branch of this family moved to Lancashire in the fourteenth century and made their seat Speke Hall, near Liverpool, which they retained until the eighteenth century, while the hall and its magnificent garden and estate are now in the care of the National Trust.

As royal courtiers, the Norreys family of Berkshire gained high honours and distinction but also became embroiled in the Wars of the Roses – the series of English civil wars that were fought in sporadic bursts between 1455 and 1487.

The antagonists were the House of Lancaster, represented by a red rose, and the House of York who were distinguished by a white rose.

Both of them cadet branches of the House of Plantagenet, the bitter and bloody struggle between them and their supporters was not finally resolved until King Richard III, of the House of York, was killed at the battle of Bosworth in August of 1485 by the Lancastrian Earl of Richmond, son of a half-brother of Henry VI.

The two claims to the throne were united as the House of Tudor when the earl assumed the throne as Henry VII and married Elizabeth of York, eldest daughter and heir of Edward IV.

Throughout all this, as prominent Lancastrians, the Norreys of Berkshire had to steer a precarious course – but managed to reach a mutually satisfactory accommodation with the House of Tudor and retained their high position in court.

Born in about 1400, Sir John Norreys, son of William Norreys of Ockwells Manor, added to his family's already impressive Berkshire holdings through his first marriage to Alice, daughter and heiress of Richard Merbrook of Yattendon and whose family seat was Yattendon Castle.

Keeper of the Wardrobe for Henry VI and with other powerful and lucrative positions including Treasurer of the Chamber and Master of the Queen's Jewels, his wife also enjoyed royal favour as Lady of the Most Noble Order of the Garter.

The fortified manor of Yattendon Castle in the Berkshire Downs was largely destroyed during the English Civil War of 1642 to 1651, and a new house built on the site in 1785.

Ockwells Manor, meanwhile, near Maidenhead, first came into the possession of the Norreys family in 1283 through Richard le (of) Norreys.

The fifteenth century house, described as 'the most refined and the most sophisticated timber-framed mansion in England', is now privately owned but still features the stained glass installed in its great hall by Sir John Norreys and showing the Coats of Arms of friends he made at court including the dukes of Somerset, Suffolk and Warwick.

He died in 1466, while one of his six sons was the Lancastrian soldier Sir William Norreys, born at Yattendon Castle in about 1441.

Knighted at the battle of Northampton in March of 1461 by Henry VI, he was one of the few Lancastrian survivors of the battle of Towton just under a year later.

He made his peace with the newly proclaimed Edward IV and was rewarded with a string of powerful appointments including, in 1468, Sheriff of Oxfordshire and Berkshire and, a year later, Esquire of the Body of the King.

But when Richard III was crowned in 1483, he reverted back to his Lancastrian sympathies.

Joining in the Duke of Buckingham's rebellion against Richard, he was forced to flee when the duke was captured at Newbury and executed.

Escaping to Brittany with a price on his head, he returned to England in the company of the Earl of Richmond and commanded a troop at the battle of Bosworth and was richly rewarded for his loyalty.

He died in 1507, while one of his grandsons was the ill-fated royal courtier Sir Henry Norris, born in about 1482 – and during whose lifetime the forms 'Norris' and 'Norreys' become confusingly interchangeable in official records and documents.

Following in the family tradition of royal service, he arrived at court as a youth and quickly became a close friend and confidante of Henry VIII, about nine years his junior.

Appointed Gentleman of the Bedchamber soon after arriving at court and, in 1526, to the archaic but nevertheless influential post of Groom of the Stool, he enjoyed a proximity to the king denied to lesser mortals.

By the time of his appointment, the role had fortunately moved on from one of sole responsibility for assisting the monarch in his ablutions and other private bodily functions to more amenable tasks including intimate discussions on royal policy.

Norris also came to enjoy friendship with the king's second wife the equally ill-fated Anne Boleyn, and was part of a court faction that supported her attempts to wield greater political power and influence and frustrate the schemes of Thomas Cromwell, Henry's powerful chief minister.

Anne fell out of favour with her mercurial husband early in 1536 and Cromwell plotted to take advantage of this in a bid to increase his own influence over the king – at the expense of his queen.

He engineered a complex conspiracy in which Norris and four other hapless courtiers were accused of having indulged in carnal relations with her and, accordingly, charged with treason.

A grand jury was assembled at Westminster Hall on May 9, 1536 and, despite the flimsiest of so-called evidence, they were found guilty and sentenced to be hanged, drawn and quartered.

But, because they had been in the service of the royal court, custom dictated this was commuted to beheading by the executioner's axe.

This was carried out on May 17 on Tower

Hill, while their reputed lover Anne Boleyn followed them to the block two days later.

Legend holds that the severed head of Norris was recovered by the family and secretly buried in the vicinity of Ockwells Manor House – which his ghost is reputed to haunt to this day.

In the acclaimed 2015 BBC television drama series *Wolf Hall*, based on the historical novels *Wolf Hall* and *Bring up the Bodies* by Hilary Mantel, Sir Henry Norris is portrayed by the actor Luke Roberts.

Despite his father's spectacular fall from grace, this did not affect the courtly career of his son Henry Norris, born in 1525. Made a Knight of the Shire for Berkshire in 1547, in 1554 he was entrusted with guarding the young Princess Elizabeth – future Queen Elizabeth I – during her lonely confinement at Woodstock, Oxfordshire.

Believing that his father had died because of his loyalty to her mother, Anne Boleyn, the queen forged a close bond of friendship with Norris and his wife Alice – whom she fondly referred to as 'Black Crow' because of her jet black hair.

It was in recognition of this loyalty and friendship that in 1566 she created him 1st Baron Norreys.

Chapter three:

Fame and infamy

Henry Norris, 1st Baron Norreys, died in 1601. He was the father of the Elizabethan soldier Sir John Norris who, despite his fame on the battlefield, also became infamous for his role in the massacre of civilians.

Born in about 1547 at Yattendon Castle and having embarked on a military career at an early age, he fought on the side of the Protestant Huguenots against the Catholics in the early years of the French Wars of Religion from 1562 to 1598.

Nicknamed 'Black Jack' by his troops – having inherited his mother's jet black hair – other theatres of war he was engaged in were the Eighty Years' War of 1566 to 1609 and the Anglo-Spanish War of 1585 to 1604 – but he is particularly remembered for brutal conduct during the Tudor Conquest of Ireland.

Frequently riven by inter-clan feuding, the island had been a ripe target in the Cambro-Norman invasion of 1169 to 1170 – with 'Cambro' denoting those aristocratic Normans who had settled in Wales following the Conquest of 1066. King Henry II claimed the island for the English Crown in 1171 with dominion ratified four years later through the Treaty of Windsor.

But the land was far from unified – there in fact being three separate 'Irelands'.

These were the territories of the privileged and powerful Norman barons and their retainers, the Ireland of the bitterly disaffected Gaelic-Irish and the Pale – comprised of Dublin, the seat of administrative power and a substantial area of its environs ruled over by an English elite.

It is from this that the expression 'to live beyond the pale' – as the native Irish had to – derives.

The Tudor Conquest of 1529 to 1603 was yet another attempt in a depressingly long series to impose the Crown's authority and quash rebellion.

In addition to military action, it also saw the implementation of a policy of 'plantation' – the settlement on lands held by the native Irish of Scottish and English subjects deemed loyal to the Crown.

With the rank of captain, Norris was serving there in 1574 under Sir Walter Devereux, Earl of Essex, when he took part in the massacre of followers of Sir Brian O'Neill after the earl invited the Irish chieftain to a banquet in Belfast.

O'Neill reciprocated the gesture by later hosting a feast in Dublin that lasted three days – but on the third day Norris and men under his command slaughtered more than 200 of his unarmed followers.

McNeill was seized and, along with his wife and others, summarily executed.

Further atrocities followed when the Earl of Essex descended on Antrim to attack the Scots-Irish chieftain Sorley Boy MacDonnell, who had established a branch of his clan there.

Before the attack got under way, MacDonnell and his fighters sent their wives, children, the sick and the aged to what he thought would be the safety of the barren fastness of Rathlin Island.

But Norris was despatched with a company of soldiers and, crossing over to the island, engaged in the mass slaughter of at least 200 of the helpless people.

It was then discovered that 'several hundred' more had hidden in caves on the shore – and they too were also massacred.

Returning to the Netherlands during the Eighty Years' War – the Dutch struggle for independence from Spain – in August of 1578 Norris was instrumental in the defeat of a Spanish force at the battle of Rijmenan, having had three horses shot from under him.

In April of the following year in a military operation that became known as the English Fury, he was in command of troops that sacked the city of Mechelen – and by which time he had become renowned for what was rather coyly described as his 'forceful leadership'.

Recalled to Ireland to take up the post of president of the province of Munster, he became severely debilitated because of battle wounds sustained over the years and complained how he had 'lost more blood in Her Majesty's service than any he knew'.

He died in Mallow, Co. Cork in September of 1597 – from what contemporaries claimed was severe depression over what he perceived as a lack of proper regard and reward for his service.

But there is a rather more sinister account of his death.

According to a young servant lad, he had seen the old warrior enter his chamber in the company of a shadowy figure.

Listening at the door, the servant claimed

Norris entered into a pact with the Devil – and when the room was opened the next morning he was found with his head and upper chest facing backwards.

In much later times, one colourfully controversial bearer of the Norris name was the businessman, politician and football club director Sir Henry Norris.

Born into a working class family in Kennington, London, in 1865, he joined a firm of solicitors when aged 14, but left after eighteen years to pursue a career in property development through the company Allen and Norris.

The business thrived by building houses in south and west London – including the Fulham area where he became director of its football club and helped to revitalise its fortunes.

Also becoming majority shareholder of Woolwich Arsenal in 1910 after the club had gone into voluntary liquidation, at one point he tried to merge it with Fulham to create a 'super club', but this was blocked by the Football League.

Undeterred, while also continuing to invest in Fulham, he moved Woolwich Arsenal to a new site at Highbury, in the north of London.

With 'Woolwich' dropped from the club's

name, the Arsenal Stadium opened in 1913 and, by 1919, they had been promoted from the Second Division to the First.

But controversy surrounded the promotion.

Arsenal had only finished fifth in the Second Division in the previous season (1914-15, since competition had been suspended throughout most of the First World War) and its promotion came at the expense of more deserving clubs that most notably included their arch rivals Tottenham Hotspur.

Although there was never any proof at the time, it was alleged the wealthy and well-connected Norris – who served from 1918 to 1922 as Conservative MP for Fulham East – had either bribed or by other means exerted influence on the Football League's voting members.

Further controversy followed in 1927 when the *Daily Mail* newspaper carried the sensational story that Norris had made 'under-the-counter' payments to Charlie Buchan, a Sunderland player, as an inducement to join Arsenal – a practice outlawed by the Football Association (FA).

Other revelations, made known following an FA investigation, were that he had used Arsenal's expense account to pay for his chauffer and even pocketed the £125 from the sale of the team bus.

Norris sued both the *Daily Mail* and the FA for libel, but the Lord Chief Justice found in their favour.

He died in 1934, while in the previous century another Henry Norris gained recognition as the leading English civil engineer who oversaw a number of lighthouse construction and repair projects.

Born in 1816 in Poplar, London, from 1869 to 1871 he was responsible for the construction of the Souter Lighthouse, the first of its kind in the world designed to be powered solely by alternating electric current.

Located at Marsden Head in South Shields, Tyne and Wear, and not deactivated until 1988, when first lit up it was described as 'without doubt one of the most powerful lights in the world.'

Also responsible for major repairs to the Eddystone Lighthouse, first constructed in 1698 off Rame Head, Plymouth and Trevose Head Lighthouse, Cornwall, he died in 1878.

Chapter four:

On the world stage

Born in 1940 in Ryan, Oklahoma, Carlos Ray Norris is the American martial artist, action movie actor, screenwriter, producer and best-selling author better known as Chuck Norris.

The holder of black belts in disciplines including Brazilian jiu jitsu, Judo and Tang Soo Do, it was after appearing in a small role in the 1969 film *The Wrecking Crew* that fellow actor and martial artist Bruce Lee encouraged him to continue acting.

Films in which he has since starred include the 1979 *A Force of One*, the 1983 *McQuade*, the 1985 *Code of Silence* and, from 2012, *The Expendables*.

Also having played the title role throughout the 1990s in the television series *Walker, Texas Ranger*, as an author his books cover a range of topics including martial arts, philosophy and Christianity and westerns.

His 1988 autobiographical *The Secret of Inner Strength: My Story* and the 2008 *Black Belt*

Patriotism: How to Reawaken America were both *New York Times* bestsellers, while his tongue-in-cheek *Chuck Norris Facts* has been a hit on the Internet since 2005.

On British shores **Hermione Norris** is the actress who first rose to fame for her role from 1998 to 2003 of Kate Marsden in the comedy drama television series *Cold Feet*.

Born in 1967 in Paddington, London, she also co-starred from 2002 to 2005 in the drama series *Wire in the Blood* and, from 2005 to 2009, in the spy series *Spooks*.

On both the small screen and big screen, **Luke Norris**, born in 1985 in Romford, London, is the actor best known for his role of Dr Dwight Enys in the television costume drama series *Poldark*, while film credits include the 2008 *The Duchess* and, from 2018, *Been So Long*.

Back on American shores, **Dean Norris**, born in 1963 in South Bend, Indiana, is the actor best known for his role from 2008 to 2013 of Drug Enforcement Administration agent Hank Schrader in the television series *Breaking Bad*.

Other television credits include the series *Under the Dome*, while big screen appearances include the 1989 *Lethal Weapon 2*, the 2007 *Evan Almighty* and, from 2017, *The Book of Henry*.

Back on British shores and in the world of comedy, Josiah Norris, born in 1989, is the award-winning alternative comedian and actor better known as **Joz Norris**.

Winner of the Comedians Choice Award at the Edinburgh Festival Fringe in 2019 for his show *Joz Norris is Dead: Long Live Mr Fruit Salad*, his performance in the webseries *The Backbenchers* won him the 2015 Los Angeles Webseries Festival Award for Outstanding Support Actor in a Comedy.

From comedy to art, **Ben Norris** was the American modernist painter renowned for his landscapes.

Born in 1910 in Redlands, California and a leading member of the California Watercolor School, major works he executed before his death in 2006 include *The Other Edge of the Clearing* and *Shadow Play*.

Known for his landscapes of the Welsh countryside, **Charles Norris** was the topographical etcher and author born in London in 1779.

Moving to Wales when aged in his early

'twenties and settling in Tenby, he became noted not only for his etchings but also as a recorder of the medieval buildings of Pembrokeshire.

Author of works including *A Historical Account of Tenby*, he died in 1858.

In a much different artistic genre, **Paul Leroy Norris** was the American comic book artist best known as co-creator in 1941 of the DC Comics superhero Aquaman.

Born in 1914 in Greenville, Ohio, it was along with writer Mort Weisinger that he created Aquaman, while he later also drew stories for Tarzan of jungle fame and, for Dell Comics, Space Cadet; he died in 2007.

From art to the equally creative world of the written word, **Charles Gilman Norris** was the American journalist, playwright and novelist born in Chicago in 1881.

Ahead of his time in many ways, a number of his novels such as the 1919 *Salt*, the 1921 *Brass: A Novel of Marriage* and the 1944 *Flint* explore such issues as the environment, ethics and birth control, while F. Scott Fitzgerald was among his literary peers and admirers.

He died in 1945, while his wife was the

prolific novelist and newspaper columnist **Kathleen Thompson Norris**, born in 1880.

From 1911 to 1959 one of the most widely read and highest paid female writers in the United States, her stories and columns appeared in publications including *The American Magazine*, *Atlantic* and *Woman's Home Companion*.

She died in 1966, while her brother-in-law was Benjamin Franklin Norris, the journalist and novelist better known as **Frank Norris**.

Born in Chicago in 1870, before his death at the age of only 32 he penned noted works including the 1899 *McTeague: A Story of San Francisco* and the 1901 *The Octopus: A Story of California*.

Still on a literary note, **George Leslie Norris** was the poet and short story writer born in 1921 in Merthyr Tydfil, South Wales.

Later settling in the United States, where he was professor of creative writing at Brigham Young University in Provo, Utah and author of collections including the 1967 *Finding Gold*, he died in 2006.

From poetry to music, Charles Eldridge Norris was the acclaimed American jazz and blues guitarist born in 1921 in Kansas City, Missouri and better known as **Chuck Norris**.

Much in demand as a session musician and having worked with performers including Little Richard and Dinah Washington, he died in 1989.

Nine years before his death, meanwhile, he recorded his solo album *The Los Angeles Flash* in Gothenburg, Sweden.

Bearers of the Norris name have also excelled in the highly competitive world of sport.

In wrestling, Anthony Norris, better known by his ring name **Ahmed Johnson**, is the American retired wrestler born in 1963 in Lake Alfred, Florida.

Known for his appearances from 1995 to 1998 with the World Wrestling Federation (WWF), he is the first African-American to have won a singles championship in the WWF.

Still in the wrestling ring, **Charlie Norris**, born in 1965 in Red Lake, Minnesota is the American retired wrestler of World Championship Wrestling (WCW) who was a five-time heavyweight champion and two-time tag team champion.

In motor racing, **Lando Norris**, born in Bristol in 1999 to an English father and Belgian mother, is the British-Belgian driver and former member of the McLaren Young Driver Programme who won the 2017 Formula 3 European Championship.

From motor racing to ice hockey, **James E. Norris** was the Canadian-American businessman who founded a dynasty of influential figures in the sport.

Born in 1879 in Montreal, he was aged 18 when his father moved one of his business interests, Norris Grain, to Chicago and which, with Norris as president, in the 1930s became the largest grain buyer in the world.

A keen hockey fan, he came to own the Detroit Red Wings of the National Hockey League and also acquired major interests in the New York Rangers and Chicago Blackhawks.

An inductee of the Hockey Hall of Fame, he died in 1952 while his business and hockey interests have been carried on by his sons and daughter.

Setting a record in sporting endeavour in May of 2010, **Bonita Norris** became when aged 22 the youngest British woman to reach the summit of Mount Everest.

Born in Wokingham, Berkshire, in 1988, she also became the first British woman to reach the summit of Mt. Lohse, the fourth highest mountain in the Himalayas – while her Everest record was broken the same month by fellow British climber, 19-year-old Leanna Shuttleworth.

One particularly heroic bearer of the Norris name is the British Army soldier and medical orderly **Michelle Norris** – aptly nicknamed 'Chuck Norris' after the action film hero.

But while the actor's exploits are in the realms of celluloid fiction, those for which she was awarded the Military Cross (MC) for bravery were in the real-life setting of the war in Iraq.

Aged just nineteen and having only recently completed basic training, she had been serving as a combat medical technician attached to the 1st Battalion Princess of Wales's Royal Regiment when she carried out the action for which she was awarded the MC.

During a search operation in Al Amarah on June 11, 2006, her company came under heavy fire and, regardless of her own safety, she dragged Colour Sergeant Ian Page to a Warrior Patrol vehicle after he was shot by a sniper.

Braving sustained fire including a bullet that shattered a radio next to her leg, she tended the sergeant's wounds until a British Lynx helicopter flown by Captain William Chesarek of the United States Marine Corps (USMC) managed to make a perilous descent and evacuate them to safety.

Later promoted from private to lance corporal, Norris was awarded her medal personally by the Queen on March 11, 2007, at the same time as Captain Chesarek – who had been serving with the British Army as part of an officer exchange programme – was awarded the Distinguished Flying Cross (DFC) for his actions.